GOD MADE ME
IN HIS
IMAGE

Helping Children
Appreciate Their Bodies

Justin S. Holcomb
& Lindsey A. Holcomb

Illustrated by
Trish Mahoney

On the bus all of the students were buzzing about their field trip to the safari park at the zoo. Everyone was excited except Ruthie and Mateo, who sat next to each other with sour faces.

"What happened to you?"
Ruthie asked her friend.

"This morning my brother
called me Big Ears,"
said Mateo.

Ruthie frowned.
"That stinks. But at least you don't have red frizzy hair and freckles.
I wish I had smooth hair and no freckles."

Just then Mrs. Chen clapped to get everyone's attention.
"Class, listen up! Since we've been reading Genesis and studying God's creation, I know we're all excited to explore the zoo."

Everyone cheered, and Mrs. Chen continued.

"The Bible tells us everything that exists was created by God—"

"Even me!" exclaimed Bobby, bouncing in his seat.

Mrs. Chen smiled.
"Yes, God created you, Bobby.
He created each and every one of you—
and the animals we're about to see today.
Why do you think he created all of us?"

Bobby stopped bouncing.
"I don't know," he said.

"The Bible says God's creation teaches people about who God is—
his power, strength, and beauty. And when we explore God's
creation, we learn about ourselves too," said Mrs. Chen.

"Who remembers the list of everything God made?" asked Mrs. Chen.

OH!

Tinaya raised her hand high. "He made light and space."

☀ SUN

🌙 MOON

★ STARS

● LIGHT

"Very good! What else did God make?"

"He made the sun, moon, stars, and other planets," said Joey.

I wish God had made me as pretty as a star, thought Ruthie. She tucked her hair behind her ear and looked down.

"That's right!" said the teacher.

"And he made the sky and seas, and he filled them with birds and fish. He also made land and plants, and he filled the earth with animals and humans. **Do you remember the word God used to describe what he made?"**

"I do!" shouted Bobby.
"He said it was 'good.'"

"That's right," said Mrs. Chen. "After each day of creation, God looked at his creation—everything from light to land to living creatures—and called it 'good.'"

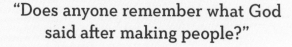

"Does anyone remember what God said after making people?"

"He said, 'My creation is now *very* good!'" said Ruthie, looking up for a moment.

"Who did God make people like?" asked Mrs. Chen.

"God said, 'Let us make man in our image,'" said Mateo. "So I guess we are somehow like God?"

"Yes," said Mrs. Chen. **"We reflect God in special ways like nothing else in creation."**

"Long ago when Genesis was written, the world was full of images—what today we would call statues. The most important statues were of kings. Each king had statues put all over their kingdoms to remind everyone that they were important and in charge.

"Just as human kings made images to remind everyone of their might,
**God, the King of the whole world,
made humans to reveal his majesty.**

**This shows the great dignity
of all human beings."**
Mrs. Chen smiled at all of her students.

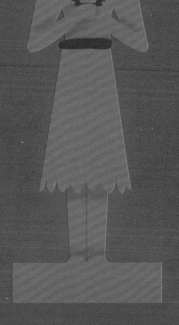

Bobby raised his hand. "Mrs. Chen, what does 'dignity' mean?"

**"Good question! When we say people have dignity,
that means they are worthy of honor and respect."**

Ruthie frowned. That didn't sound like the way she felt today.
She leaned in to hear Mrs. Chen better.

"So we are God's royal images?" asked Ruthie.

"That's right," said Mrs. Chen. "Psalm 139 says,
'You created the deepest parts of my being. You put me together inside
my mother's body. How you made me is amazing and wonderful. I praise you
for that. What you have done is wonderful. I know that very well.'"*

Mrs. Chen continued,
"This verse tells us God designed you himself!
God made you—all of you—on purpose.
Every part of you is wonderfully made!"

"I'm not sure my frizzy hair
and freckles are wonderful,"
Ruthie whispered to Mateo.

"Or my ears!"
Mateo whispered back.

The bus rolled to a stop, and the students began to chatter.

"Class, this is why we're taking a field trip today: to explore God's creation.
**One way we learn about God is by looking at all he made,
and that includes you!**
Let's go see the animals God made!"

Mrs. Chen led the children off the bus and introduced them to David, their safari guide. She knew David from church.

David said, "Today you are in for a big adventure! This zoo is a sanctuary for animals who were hurt in the wild and need a safe place to heal and recover. We are going to drive through the park, and I'm going to show you the 'Big Five.'"

Bobby looked up. "Who are the Big Five?"

David smiled. "Good question! The Big Five are famous African wild animals:

The

1 **Leopard**

2 **Rhinoceros**

3 **Elephant**

4 **Lion**

5 **Buffalo**

The children started talking about which
animal they most wanted to see.

"Everyone in the Jeeps. Let's go on an amazing adventure!
Remember to keep your hands and arms inside the Jeeps,
and whisper so you don't scare the animals away."

As the Jeeps jostled over bumps in the road, David announced,

"When we spot an animal, I am going to tell you some important facts about how they are made and why that's important.

"Look to your left, kids! Now this animal isn't on the Big Five list, but she is big nonetheless! Under the acacia tree you'll see the world's tallest living animal. A giraffe's height is helpful for keeping a lookout for predators, such as lions and hyenas.

The children gasped as a tall, white giraffe emerged from behind the trees.

David continued, "Zoe is so beautiful. She has leucism, which means her skin cells don't produce any color. This not only makes her different from the other animals; it also makes her more vulnerable to predators, since she doesn't have the spots that help camouflage giraffes.

"God still gave her other strengths that can keep her safe. She can use her long legs and neck to fight predators. A swift kick from one of her legs can do serious damage to a lion or hyena. She is one of a kind. Everyone always wants to get a glimpse of Zoe!"

Ruthie whispered to Mateo,
"I guess being different isn't always bad."

Mateo agreed, "Yeah, being different makes Zoe really cool. I still wish my ears were smaller and that my brother would stop reminding me how big they are."

David pointed to a tree.
"Look up and you'll see the first of the Big Five today!
Leopards hunt at night, so this leopard wants to sleep.
Unlike giraffes, leopards prefer to live and hunt alone."

David paused.
"Can anyone tell me how they're similar to giraffes?"

Bobby raised his hand and said, hesitantly,
"They have spots like giraffes?"

"That's right! God made the leopard a light color with distinctive dark
spots that are called rosettes, because they resemble the shape of a
rose. No two leopards have the same markings or color. In fact, each
leopard's spots are unique, similar to human fingerprints."

David quizzed the children again.
"But can anyone tell me why a
leopard has spots?"

After a moment or two of silence,
Ruthie raised her hand.
"Is it for camouflage, like the giraffe?"

"Yes! Giraffes have spots to hide
from predators, but God gave leopards spots
to help them hide while they're hunting."

Ruthie whispered to Mateo,
"I wonder why God gave me spots.
I wish they helped me hide, instead of making me stick out."

Mateo responded, "Stick out! Like you have anything to complain about.
My ears literally stick out."

Mrs. Chen overheard Mateo and Ruthie's conversation. "David, do we
always know the purpose behind every part of an animal's design?"

"Not at all!" David responded. "We're still discovering new things every day.
But just like in Genesis, we can trust that all of God's designs are good,
even the smallest details. The Bible also tells us God knows when a sparrow falls,
and even how many hairs we have on our heads.

**"If God knows all this, we can trust he knew what he was doing
when he put each creature together in its own unique way.
God knew what he was doing when he created each of you too."**

As they rounded a corner, David said,
"Look toward the watering hole.
Can you see the rhinos wallowing in the muddy pool?
They are the second of the Big Five animals.
They put mud all over to protect their skin
from the sun, to cool off, and remove parasites."